IMAGES
of America

SALT FORK STATE PARK

On the cover: The family of R. E. "Doc" Willis poses in front of a home that once stood near the Salt Fork park office. From left to right are Mrs. Allen (Doc's mother-in-law), Edgar Willis, Doc, Annie Willis, Clyde Willis, and Villa ? (cousin of Annie Willis). (Courtesy of Carl Allen.)

IMAGES
of America

SALT FORK STATE PARK

Meredith Bowman, William Kerrigan,
and Alicia Seng

ARCADIA
PUBLISHING

Copyright © 2007 by Meredith Bowman, William Kerrigan, and Alicia Seng
ISBN 0-7385-4133-8

Published by Arcadia Publishing
Charleston SC, Chicago IL, Portsmouth NH, San Francisco CA

Printed in the United States of America

Library of Congress Catalog Card Number: 2006934714

For all general information contact Arcadia Publishing at:
Telephone 843-853-2070
Fax 843-853-0044
E-mail sales@arcadiapublishing.com
For customer service and orders:
Toll-Free 1-888-313-2665

Visit us on the Internet at www.arcadiapublishing.com

CONTENTS

ACKNOWLEDGMENTS

We wish to express our sincere gratitude to these individuals and institutions: Barbara Allen, Carl Allen, John Baird, Ralph Bichard, Nancy Carney, Cookie Connell, Pauline Cornish, Harold Davis, Clifford and Mary Lou Eagleson, Jeff East, Melissa Essex, the Fitzgerald family, Walter Huber, Dottie King, Bonnie and Jack Landman, John Lanning, Reed Larrick, Jason Larson, Martha Martin, Alice McCance, Charlie Parker, Kent Pattison, John Reed, Don Rose, James Scott, Lori Taylor, David Thompson, Kurt Tostenson, The Daily Jeffersonian, Friends of Kennedy Stone House (KSH), Finley Local History Room in the Guernsey County Library (FLHR), Guernsey County Historical Society (GCHS), Guernsey County Map Room, and Salt Fork State Park.

Special thanks go out to Muskingum College president Anne Steele and the Board of Trustees for their continued support of the Center for Regional Planning and the Muskie Summer Fellows program, both of which made this book possible. All royalties from sales of Salt Fork State Park will go to fund the work of the Friends of the Kennedy Stone House, dedicated to preserving the stories of all Salt Fork families.

Meredith Bowman, William Kerrigan, and Alicia Seng
Department of History, Muskingum College
New Concord, August 2006

INTRODUCTION

Ohio's largest state park covers about 20,000 acres of rolling, forested terrain just eight miles northeast of Cambridge in Guernsey County. At the heart of the park lies the serpentine Salt Fork Lake, 3,000 acres of water wide and deep at its heart, but stretching its many sinuous fingers outward through forested sandstone hollows, to the base of the runs and rills that fill its basin. For the outdoorsman, the naturalist, and the explorer, Salt Fork State Park offers unlimited opportunities for tranquil encounters with nature. All that is required to get away from the bustle and noise of civilization is to take a short walk down one of the park's many trails, or a paddle into the far reaches of one of the lake's many fingers. Soon, the visitor might begin to believe they have stepped into a wilderness past.

Despite the park's timeless wilderness feel, Salt Fork State Park is as much a human-created landscape as a natural one. Artifacts from the park's ancient past—Adena and Hopewell cultures—have been unearthed on what is now park land, and Native Americans boiled water to make salt at the headwaters of the creek which gave the park its name. Early in the 19th century, migrants of English, Scots-Irish, and German stock moved into the area, rapidly transforming a thickly forested region of old growth beech, oak, maple, hickory, and chestnut trees into rolling pastures, fields, and meadows. For almost 150 years families grazed sheep, grew corn and hay, and cultivated abundant gardens and orchards on this land. They traveled on old farm roads and crossed the region's many creeks on covered bridges named after the owners of the property they crossed: Armstrong, Gunn, McCleary, Milligan, Tyner, and Yaus. They bought and sold goods at crossroads general stores in places called Brady, Clio, O'Dell, and Warnetown. They relied on water-powered gristmills to grind their grain and sawmills to cut lumber. These mills lined the Salt, Sugar Tree, Rocky, Clear, and Brushy Forks of Wills Creek. Their children were educated in one-room schoolhouses called Berwick, Crossroads, Grandridge, Independence, Knob, and Sugar Tree. On Sundays, they traveled to worship at Allen's Chapel, Center Baptist, Clear Fork Presbyterian, Irish Ridge Methodist, Pleasant Hill, Winterset, and a half dozen other lovingly maintained churches. The family names of Allen, Armstrong, Baird, Gibson, Kennedy, Lanning, Parker, Taylor, Tetrick, Warne, and many others were imprinted on this land for generations.

In the 1960s however, the state bought out the people that lived in the area to make way for the park. The new park would encompass almost all of Jefferson township, and parts of those bounding it: Madison, Monroe, Wills, Center, and Liberty. An earthen dam was completed in 1967, and within a few years, once-fertile bottomlands lay at the bottom of a man-made lake. Over time, new forest has reclaimed fields and pastures, and wildlife has returned in abundance.

The state dismantled most of the homesteads, mills, bridges, and churches that lay within the park's boundaries, but the evidence of their presence is still discernable to the observant explorer. One unique structure was left alone: a house constructed of large sandstone blocks, built by Benjamin and Margaret Kennedy in 1840. For many years, the Kennedy Stone House stood silently above the waters of Sugar Tree Fork, disappearing into the new forest by late spring each year, as the trees leafed out. In 2000, local residents—many with family ties to the region—began to restore the house, and it is now open as a living history museum, telling the story of the Kennedys and all of the other families who once made a life on these lands. *Salt Fork State Park* celebrates the human heritage of the parklands, and tells the story of the land's transformation into the park today. It offers the park visitor a glimpse into the lives, labor, and leisure of the park's past residents, and points the curious explorer toward some of the many remnants of the park's agrarian past.

One

LIFE IN THE
SALT FORK REGION

Since the first arrival of white settlers at the beginning of the 19th century, the Salt Fork region was an area mostly populated by farmers. The day-to-day lives of the early settlers were shaped by the chores of farming, such as raising sheep and cattle. Additionally they grew crops, like hay and wheat. Most of the farms in the region were strung along the many creeks that meandered through the region, including the Salt, Sugar Tree, Brushy, and Rocky Forks. There were also various gristmills and sawmills that rose up along these creeks, to take advantage of the natural power of the water contained within them. The largest mill in the area was located along Wills Creek at Liberty, later known as Kimbolton. Other mills also appeared, such as McCleary's, Linn's, and Armstrong's. Although there were no towns of any substantial size in the region, residents encountered each other at the various crossroads towns in the area, such as Clio, Brady, Winterset, and Odell. There were often general stores at these towns, where people could do their household shopping, pick up their mail, and engage in social interaction with seldom-seen neighbors. These general stores began to fade as improved roads provided access to larger towns. One former resident recalled the last days of these general stores, noting that one could always find a few loafers idling away the evening on the front porch, playing checkers. Most of the region was quiet and removed from larger society, but in the southern areas along old Route 22, one could encounter a bit more traffic as farmers drove their livestock to city markets. Stewart's Tavern in Winterset was a popular stopping place for these drivers, where they could pen their livestock behind the tavern and seek rest for the night.

The Salt Fork region was defined by the many tributaries that flowed through its valleys, carving fertile but flood-prone bottomlands in their path. The longest of these—Salt Fork Creek—meandered in a northwesterly direction from its headwaters near a salt spring in present day Wills township across Jefferson, Center, and Liberty townships, until it merged with Wills Creek, south of the village of Liberty (Kimbolton). The creeks provided waterpower for essential gristmills and sawmills, and many of the region's roads also followed along the routes carved by water over the centuries. (Courtesy of FLHR.)

Life for most of the region's subsistence-oriented farmers was simple and austere. Labor was scarce, and resources limited. This pigpen, which makes use of the natural rock ledge to keep the swine contained, is one example of the subsistence farmer's make-do ingenuity. The split rail fence that completes the pen was commonly used on subsistence-oriented farms, as it could be constructed with family labor, using readily available resources. (Courtesy of FLHR.)

Not all of the agricultural activity in the region was focused on subsistence. The most important commercial agricultural activity in the area was raising sheep—specifically the merino—prized for their wool. More than any other factor, world demand for merino wool was the primary driver of settlement into the area in the early decades of the 19th century. Early families like the Parkers and Kennedys arrived in the region seeking grazing land for merino. (Courtesy of Charlie Parker.)

Every spring, the sheep on area farms were sheared before they could naturally shed their wool. The wool was then sold to companies to be processed and made into clothing and other household goods. An unidentified man assists John Taylor in this lengthy process the year this photograph was taken. (Courtesy of Lori Taylor.)

Families grew corn, beans, wheat, and other crops, in addition to raising livestock. Farm tractors and other combustion-powered machinery became more common in the region after World War II and greatly aided the planting and harvesting of crops. Charlie Parker, pictured here in 1949 with his corn picker, was crowned the Corn Growing Champion of Guernsey County. (Courtesy of Charlie Parker.)

Some farms continued to rely on traditional methods even after World War II. The Eagleson family cane mill was operated by attaching two horses to the end of a big pole, then walking them in a circle so the two big-toothed gears could grind the sorghum. Bernard, the youngest of the 13 Eagleson children, perches here on the pummy (pomace) pile, while Melvin and Irene Jackson pose in front. (Courtesy of Clifford Eagleson.)

Mr. and Mrs. Ray Gibson sit in their buggy in the early 1900s, outside of the general store at Brady. By the 1930s, improved roads, increased automobile ownership, and rural free delivery made general stores, such as the one at Brady, less essential to the lives of farmers. Brady General Store was one of the oldest business establishments in Guernsey County. Its proprietors over the years included, Mr. Naphtali, Mr. Ferbrache, Samuel Thomas, Burlingame and Wood, James H. Warne, and William A. McCullough. (Courtesy of GCHS.)

The Brady General Store stood along what is now Road 14 to Salt Fork Marina. The proprietor opened the store at daylight and closed when the last customer left. Thursdays and Saturdays were big days for people to come into the store, and gave isolated farmers an opportunity to visit with neighbors. The store also served as a post office, polling station, and meeting place for school trustees. (Courtesy of GCHS.)

14

Times did begin to change in the region in the years after World War II. The combustion engine slowly replaced the work previously done by water and livestock. This gas-powered sawmill operated near the crossroads town of Brady in October 1946. (Courtesy of FLHR.)

Clio was a crossroads town, located near Armstrong's Mill in Jefferson Township. The location of the community was just north of where the camper's beach is today. There was a post office and general store located there for families to buy goods. (Courtesy of GCHS.)

The town of Liberty (now Kimbolton) resides on Wills Creek west of the parklands. The mill in this picture was built in 1847 by Julius McCleary, Joseph Brow, and William Frame. Matthew Kennedy bought the mill in 1900 and made improvements and additions, until it was considered one of the best mills in the county. In October 1908, the mill burned to the ground, and Kennedy's uninsured loss amounted to about $15,000. (Courtesy of KSH.)

The third Kimbolton Mill and bridge stands here in August 1946. This structure was built on the original foundations of the second Kimbolton Mill, run by Matthew Kennedy, which had burned to the ground in 1908. (Courtesy of KSH.)

Linn's Mill was located on Salt Fork Creek, behind today's park office. It was built by George Linn as early as 1814 and was run by the Linn family. (Courtesy of GCHS.)

James Bratton, the first settler in Madison Township, established a home in 1805 on Brushy Fork Creek at the present site of Winterset. He kept a tavern in the Winchester area, as the town was known at the time. He and his wife had 11 children, and in 1812, the family moved to the Pleasant Hill community in Jefferson Township. (Courtesy of GCHS.)

The crossroads town of Winterset is located in Madison Township, just east of the borders of the park, though many residents who used to reside within the boundaries of the park frequented the establishments in Winterset. The Elias Tetrick home, located half a mile west of Winterset, was a stop on the Underground Railroad, between Senacaville and Gnadenhutten. (Courtesy of FLHR.)

Stewarts General Store at Winterset, located in the southern portion of the park in Center Township, was a common meeting place for area farmers. The store supplied all the basic needs of the local community, thereby saving them from making the more difficult journey into Cambridge. (Courtesy of GCHS.)

Stewarts Tavern in Winterset stands here in the early 1900s. This structure is still standing today and serves as a residence to Pauline Cornish, who founded the Friends of the Kennedy Stone House organization in 1999. (Courtesy of GCHS.)

The Chiesa Fruit Stand was located along U.S. Route 21 in North Salem, Liberty Township. Many Salt Fork families sold their produce through this market. (Courtesy of FLHR.)

Rocky Fork was a small crossroads town in southern portion of Monroe Township. The Rocky Fork Creek, one of the northern most waterways in the Salt Fork area, flowed nearby. (Courtesy of GCHS.)

Two

FAMILIES

The Salt Fork region contained ample farmland that provided sustenance and shelter for generations of families, from the time of the earliest arrivals until the 1960s. Some prominent families, like the Allens, Parkers, and Bairds, arrived in the first decade of the 19th century. Many more families followed in their wake, some coming from as far away as the British Isles and Germany. Others migrated from places much closer, such as Pennsylvania or Cadiz, Ohio, along the Old Steubenville Road. The broad, fertile bottom lands of the region, punctuated by rolling hills, lured farmers to the area. The bottoms were excellent for growing crops; the hillsides, once cleared, were ideal for grazing livestock. In fact, it was the economic opportunities provided by the demand for merino wool, more than any other factor that directed settlement in the region. Shepherding did not require flat land, and in the newly opened United States Military District, land was available for $2 an acre. The families that lived in the region were generally large, and as soon as children were old enough, they assisted with the myriad chores inherent to farm life. Patriarchs saved to acquire land for their progeny, and this resulted in clustered tracts of land controlled by members of a single family, as in the case of the Warnetown area in southern Jefferson Township. Many of these well-established families farmed the same land for five generations, passing ownership down through their children and living on the same plot of land all their lives. The families who once resided within the current borders of the park were displaced by the state during the 1950s and 1960s for the creation of the lake and park. The following chapter offers a glimpse into the lives of just a few of the many families who made their lives in the Salt Fork region.

In 1806, William Allen, born in Yorkshire, England, arrived in the Salt Fork region, eventually amassing a 750-acre farm. The Allen family was among the first families to settle in Jefferson township, establishing the first church in the Allen home a short time later. Here in the summer of 2006, generations of Allens returned to the site of their former farm for a reunion. (Courtesy of Carl Allen.)

Vandimond "Dima" Allen with his hives is pictured here. Dima lived in the region from 1857 to 1947. A pious man, he never swore, drank, or chased women, and was easy to please. Bee-keeping was a common practice among Salt Fork farmers. The honey was a valued sweetener, and beeswax was useful for making candles in the days before electric lights. (Courtesy of Carl Allen.)

The Allens raised corn, wheat, potatoes, strawberries, clover, and timothy hay on this land for more than 150 years. One of the Allen's three barns is pictured on the right. The small structure in the center background is on the approximate location of today's park office. (Courtesy of Carl Allen.)

Here Lorain Allen is seen cultivating corn in 1947, with his horses Dock and Dan. The bottom lands along the creek were rich land for cultivation, but also susceptible to flooding. This picture is taken near the spot where the main park road first crosses Salt Fork, north of the park headquarters. (Courtesy of Carl Allen.)

Carl Allen, in his younger days, is hoeing seedling corn on the Allen bottomlands in 1947. (Courtesy of Carl Allen.)

Allen, seen here in 2005, surveys the lands that were once his family farm. Their home was located where the ranger station is now located. He still resides near the park. (Courtesy of The Daily Jeffersonian.)

Mary Alma Ford McCance was born in the early 1900s and grew up within the boundaries of the present park on the Ford family farm. Her younger brother, John E. Ford, born in 1907, died in infancy at only 10 months and 11 days old. Originally buried in the Allen Church Cemetery, near park headquarters, his grave was relocated to the Pleasant Hill Cemetery when the park was created. (Courtesy of Martha Martin.)

Martha Ford was the daughter of William Logan Ford from his first marriage. She is pictured here with her half-brother, Earl Ford. Martha later married Henry Armstrong, and the couple lived on a farm within the borders of the park with their two children, Robert and Helen. Earl married twice, and it was with his second wife, Erma, that he fathered their two daughters, Peggy and Imogene. (Courtesy of Martha Martin.)

William Logan Ford and his eldest daughter, Martha Ford, pose for a portrait around 1900. William believed that the education of his children was important above all else. In 1919, he moved his family off of their farm in Salt Fork to a farm that was located much closer to Muskingum College. He is listed among those who donated money for the construction of Cambridge Hall on the college's campus. (Courtesy of Martha Martin.)

William and Sadie Ford were married February 13, 1902. The couple is pictured here in 1952, long after they had sold their farm and moved from the Salt Fork area. William was said to have been very good with horses, and he also raised merino sheep on his farm in Salt Fork. (Courtesy of Martha Martin.)

William Robert Armstrong was the child of Henry and Martha Armstrong, and the grandson of William Logan Ford. The young boy is pictured here around 1928, on the Armstrong homestead in Jefferson Township. (Courtesy of Martha Martin.)

Roy Baird, age 21, sits with his brother John, age 1, on his lap in 1915. Shortly after this picture was taken, Roy was paralyzed in a farm accident. He died in 1920, at the age of 26. (Courtesy of John Baird.)

Russell "Bakes" Jones dug the pond at the Roy Ewing farm using his Old Fordson tractor in 1930. To give the tractor more traction, cement was attached to the wheels. As a young man, John Baird worked for the Ewing brothers on this farm picking fruit. Offered 50¢ a day or one penny per quart, John chose the latter and often managed to pick 100 quarts of strawberries in a day. (Courtesy of John Baird.)

A mature John Baird stands with his arm around Bill Pollock, a well-known North Salem blacksmith, at a picnic in Jefferson Township. After taking a bride, John and his new wife, Eva, purchased a Salt Fork farm in 1936. They could produce 1,200 bushels of oat from six acres of bottomland and sold the milk from their dairy cattle through the Guernsey County Milk Producers Association. John's farming career ended abruptly in 1954, when a lightning strike on his barn injured him and most of his cattle. John and Eva moved into town shortly after the accident. (Courtesy of John Baird.)

Dwight Eagleson stands with Ben Stinett in front of the Eagleson home in Madison township. Eagleson's parents, Rev. Alexander "Bo" Eagleson and Laura Finney Eagleson, purchased this 160-acre farm for $1,800 in 1878; the family house was constructed on the land in 1910. In 1918, Dwight Eagleson moved onto the farm with his wife, Gustava McIntire Eagleson, to care for his parents and to raise their children. Dwight and Gustava remained on the property until the state purchased their farm in 1961, when they moved into Cambridge. (Courtesy of Clifford Eagleson.)

Dwight and Gustava Eagleson stand on the farm in 1924 with their fifth child, Helen Ione Eagleson. The Eaglesons had 13 children: 11 sons and 2 daughters. All 11 sons served in the armed forces overseas, and all 11 returned safely home. The Veterans Memorial Courtyard at the Kennedy Stone House contains bricks bearing the names of all the Eaglesons who have served their country. (Courtesy of Clifford Eagleson.)

Dwight Eagleson, seated, holds son Clifford while daughter Helen stands at his side. Cliff played basketball and ran track at Madison High School. When school was out, all the Eagelsons pitched in with the farm chores. During Christmas vacations, he and his brothers would help their father cut coal mine posts from the hardwood trees on their land to help support their large family. (Courtesy of Clifford Eagleson.)

From left to right, Cliff, Helen, Hervey, Charles Craig, Earl "Eddie" Edmond, Donald Lester, and Walter Irving Eagleson pose with their lunch pails before their first day of school at Grand Ridge in September 1937. A typical school day for the children began at dawn with their morning farm chores and then a hearty breakfast, before walking 1.75 miles to their school with a jam sandwich in their lunch pails. (Courtesy of Clifford Eagleson.)

Jack and Bonnie Landman's farm, pictured here in 1954, was located along old U.S. Route 22, about a half mile from today's park entrance. They raised livestock and a variety of crops. The family dearly loved their farm and, like many residents, fought the sale of their property to the state. The Landmans were among the very last to vacate, leaving the property in 1967. (Courtesy of Jack and Bonnie Landman.)

Jack Landman stands with one of his bulls on the 125-acre family farm in 1950. The couple milked dairy cattle for the first four or five years that they lived on their farm, then switched to beef cattle and hogs. (Courtesy of Jack and Bonnie Landman.)

Tim Landman, son of Jack and Bonnie Landman, is held by his grandfather Wheeler Landman on the family farm in Jefferson Township, August 1957. (Courtesy of Jack and Bonnie Landman.)

The Landman's dog, Duke, stands in front of a building on the Landman farm, which was used as a shop and storage. The structure had originally been a general store in the crossroads town of Clio and was later moved to the Landman's farm. (Courtesy of Jack and Bonnie Landman.)

Bonnie Landman stands in the yard on the family farm in 1966. It was only one year later that the couple finally relinquished control of their land to the state for the construction of Salt Fork Lake and park. Bonnie recalls with sadness the sound of the front door closing on the empty house as she walked away for the last time. (Courtesy of Jack and Bonnie Landman.)

The Landman children are enjoying an unconventional bike ride around the family farm. The twin girls, Cindy and Sandy, are perched behind their younger brother, Tim, who had been given control of the pedals. The Landman children attended grade school and high school in Madison while living in Jefferson Township. These schools were located between Antrim and Winterset. Both buildings are now gone. (Courtesy of Jack and Bonnie Landman.)

In 1958, the Charles Fitzgerald farm presented a picturesque view of Beeham Road, bordering what is now the southeast corner of the park. Most of this land today is covered in forest. In the rear high ground was a Kennedy farm, though not the same farm that held the Kennedy Stone House. (Courtesy of David Thompson.)

Members of the Fitzgerald family, along with friends, come in from the fields after a day of farming in 1964. Dan and Bill Garner pace to the left of the tractor, while Pearly Fitzgerald and John Johnson are on the tractor and wagon. To the right, John Fitzgerald walks with Tom Garner and marsha Fitzgerald, while Janet Fitzgerald poses on a bale of hay. (Courtesy of the Fitzgerald family.)

Walter and Barbara Larrick were married in the Salt Fork area in 1903. Walter was a miner in the Rigby mine for three years, while Barbara came from a family of wagon sellers. There was a mine located on their home property for many years. (Courtesy of Reed Larrick.)

The Larrick family lived in Jefferson Township from 1935 to 1960. At one point, they lived near the Kennedys and purchased 150 acres from Don Kennedy. On their property stood the family house and two barns for their livestock. (Courtesy of Reed Larrick.)

Noah Larrick kneels to the left of his brother, Reed, in the 1940s. With Reed is his first coon dog, Blue, who helped him catch his three raccoons that season. (Courtesy of Reed Larrick.)

Reed stands in his present home a few miles south of the park in 2006. In his hands is the first gun he ever purchased—the same gun that was with him in the previous photograph. He purchased it 75 years ago for $12 and has kept it in working order ever since. (Courtesy of William Kerrigan.)

John B. Larrick kneels next to the family hunting dog, Blue, in the early 1940s. All male members of the family liked to hunt, and there were years in the 1920s that they might be able to receive as much as $25 for one raccoon hide. (Courtesy of Reed Larrick.)

Reed Larrick was a member of the local Coon Hunters Association for many years. Reed enjoyed hunting raccoons and owned many prize winning hounds. Here is Reed with his nephew John Lanning, and their hunting dogs Salt Fork Jennie and her daughter, Salt Fork Sue. (Courtesy of Reed Larrick.)

Walter Larrick poses with his 12-year-old hunting dog, Buster, in the early 1940s. Walter and his dog had caught 12 raccoons that season. (Courtesy of Reed Larrick.)

Barbara and Walter Larrick were married for over 50 years. Together they had nine children. This picture was taken on their golden anniversary. Pictured from left to right are (first row) Mary, Barbara, Walter, and Hazel; (second row) Reed, Margaret, John, Fannie, Noah "Pat," Peggy, and Dave. (Courtesy of Reed Larrick.)

Alexander Luzadder (1824–?), the grandson of Abraham Luzadder, lived in the Salt Fork area before moving to Indiana with his wife, Margaret Askins Garey. The Luzadder family poses for a portrait at their home in Indiana in 1906. From left to right are (first row) Glenn Crim, James R. Marshall, Lauretta Crim, Lois Marshall, and Gail Marshall; (second row) Florence Luzadder Pickard, Gilbert Luzadder, Lillian Luzadder Marshall, and Homer Luzadder; (third row) Dr. John E. Luzadder, Grant Luzadder, Margaret Luzadder, Maude Luzadder, Alexander Luzadder, Sophie Luzadder Floyd, and James B. Marshall, holding Ruth Marshall. (Courtesy of Nancy Owens.)

The grave of Abraham Luzadder (1757–1826), a Revolutionary War veteran and Salt Fork resident, is marked by two stones. The flat stone was set by the Daughters of the American Revolution in 1939, while the upright stone was later established by the government at the request of David Luzadder. Abraham's farm was located just off Beeham Run Road near the present day entrance to the park. Abraham was rumored to have accumulated a great deal of gold in his lifetime, which he kept in an iron pot. One night, the homestead was threatened by a band of roving Native Americans, and he took the pot into the woods and hid it. He never told anyone the location of the gold, and on his deathbed, he uttered just a few words to hint at its location before passing. The family has searched for the gold through generations, but no one has ever found it. (Courtesy of Marilyn Lundquist.)

Ira O. Nelson sits in a 1928 Ford Roadster. Ira was the son of Samuel C. Nelson and Pearl Barthalow Nelson, who had bought the family farm around 1915 from the Valentines. Ira was a self-employed carpenter and cabinet builder. He later married Maxine (Salsa) Nelson. He is buried in Pleasant Hill Cemetery. The old Nelson property on Larrick Ridge is now under water. (Courtesy of KSH.)

The Nelson homestead is believed to be the property where the last Native American of Jefferson Township was murdered. According to the legend, George Launtz, a veteran of the War of 1812, recognized a local Native American as one who participated in the Copus massacre near Mansfield. Launtz plotted to murder him by befriending the Native American, getting him drunk, and pushing him off a cliff into the swollen Salt Fork, south of the present-day lodge. Launtz allegedly confessed for the murder to his family on his deathbed. (Courtesy of KSH.)

John Marling fell for Mary Alice Tidrick in 1941, after hearing her sing at Clear Fork Baptist Church. Though he was immediately smitten with her, they did not marry until June 1948. Here they stand in front of their house on the farm in the early 1950s, with the first three of their eight children, Connie, Sharon, and Russell. (Courtesy of KSH.)

Curtis Marling, the fourth child of John and Mary Alice Marling, stands behind a Pontiac belonging to his grandfather Arthur Marling. In the background stands the family barn and silo on their farm. (Courtesy of KSH.)

The eight children of the Marlings pose for a picture in 1963 on the family farm in Jefferson Township. From left to right are, (first row) Russell, William, Dean, Mark, and Curtis; (second row) Connie, holding Nancy, and Sharon. (Courtesy of KSH.)

Though the Marling family moved from their farm in Jefferson Township in 1966 to a farm in Muskingum County, they returned to Salt Fork State Park to take a scenic boat ride on the lake, over the spot where their farm was once located. Pictured from left to right are Connie, Sharon, Curtis, Russell, Mary Alice, John, Nancy, William, Mark, and Dean. (Courtesy of KSH.)

John and Fannie Parker emigrated from New Jersey to Jefferson Township in 1818, making them the first of five generations of Parkers to live in the Salt Fork area. Their son, John S. Parker, built the Parker home in 1867, where three generations of Parkers would later be born. Charles E. Parker, a son born in 1877 to John S. Parker, stands in front of the family home in February 1906 with his wife, Rena McCullough Parker. (Courtesy of Charlie Parker.)

Charles Parker (1877–1932) stands on a hillside at the farm, feeding his Dorset sheep in 1915. Since Dorset sheep were hot breeders and would produce young out of season, they were an ideal breed for the lamb market that flourished in the holiday season. Charles never had working dogs to herd the sheep in from the fields; he would instead call them in by shaking a bucket full of corn. All of the Parkers raised sheep on their farm, and with the exception of Charles Parker, the breed of choice for every generation was Delaine merino. (Courtesy of Charlie Parker.)

Rena McCullough Parker feeds chickens and ducks at the farm in 1927. The Parkers raised Rhode Island Reds and possibly leghorn chickens on their farm, in addition to short-horned cattle and sheep. (Courtesy of Charlie Parker.)

John "Willis" Parker, son of Charles Parker, was the first Parker to own a tractor; he purchased an F12 Farmall in 1941. His son Charlie, seated all the way to the right, often drove the tractor around the farm, as he was doing here in 1946. He is accompanied by Pal, their dog, and two neighbor boys Sam and Ed Patterson. (Courtesy of Charlie Parker.)

Tractor rides on the Parker farm remained fairly common throughout the years. John "Willis" Parker gives his grandsons, Jeffrey and Stephen Parker, a cruise around the barn in 1964. (Courtesy of Charlie Parker.)

In its final months of ownership by the Parker family, the farm appeared as it did here in June 1966. The state purchased the 257-acre farm from John Willis and Eva Parker in 1966 for the development of the park, effectively ending their five-generation reign over the land. (Courtesy of Charlie Parker.)

The McCullough-Parker family poses for a portrait in 1933. From left to right are (first row, including children seated on the laps) George Bell, Donald Rose, Joan Rose, Gene Rose, Beard Rose, and Bob Rose; (second row) John Willis Parker holding baby Charlie, Leonard Warden, John McCullough, Ed Bell, Sam Warden, Len McCleary, Frank McCullough, Clarence Warden, Burt Rose; (third row) Lee Bell, Grace Parker, Eva Parker, Ruth Bell, Lula McCullough, Edith Adams, Doris McCullough, Mary McCullough, Flora Proctor, Lena Baird, Alice Warden, Ella Adams, Bell Warden, Bernice Warden, Rena Parker, Mary Warden, Margaret Fisher, Mary Rose, Nan Bell, Ernest "Ernie" Warden, and unidentified. (Courtesy of Charlie Parker.)

John Wiggins Taylor (1852–1927) and his wife, Anna Bell Baird Taylor (1852–1930), pose for a family portrait with their children in the 1890s. Bertha Taylor Patterson (1878–1953), Lena Taylor Warne (1882–1978), Wilmer Taylor (1886–1964), and Flora Taylor Tedrick (1888–1973) were the four Taylor children to survive to adulthood. Anna gave birth to a fifth child, David Ralph Taylor (1890–1891), who died as an infant. He is buried in McCleary Cemetery, and his gravestone still stands today. (Courtesy of Lori Taylor.)

John and Anna Taylor sit with their dog on the front porch of their home in Salt Fork. They lived out their lives as farmers in the northern part of the park, between Sugar Tree and Rocky Forks, in section 24 of Monroe Township. (Courtesy of Lori Taylor.)

John and Anna Taylor used their horse-drawn buggy as their primary means of transportation throughout the Salt Fork area. Long after the advent of the automobile, many Salt Fork families continued to rely on horses and their own feet for travel between farm and town. (Courtesy of Lori Taylor.)

Edwin "Eddie" B. Taylor was the brother of John W. Taylor and resided on the Taylor land, in an area known as Taylor Hollow. Though the house no longer stands on the land, the cornerstones for the structure still exist to this day in their original locations. (Courtesy of Lori Taylor.)

Bert Ray Tedrick guides his yoke of oxen, which he had raised from calves, on the farm of George Willis. In the back of the wagon stands Bert's cousin, Ralph Willis. Bert married Flora Taylor, the fourth child of John and Anna Taylor, in 1910. Bert was raised and worked on the George Willis farm. (Courtesy of Lori Taylor.)

Bertha Taylor Patterson, the eldest child of John and Anna Taylor, stands with her husband, Gus Patterson, on their farm with their two grandchildren, David and Robert Gass. In back of them, Eddie Taylor lounges next to his horse while Edwin Gass leans against the barn. Edwin married the Patterson's daughter, Geneva, and was the father of David and Robert. Directly behind them, in the background, is where Salt Fork's main lodge stands today. (Courtesy of Lori Taylor.)

Bill Pollock was the resident blacksmith at North Salem for a number of years. Though serious about his work, Pollock was said to be quite the jokester with his family and friends. (Courtesy of John Baird.)

Esther Nelson was married to Pollock. She supported her husband's trade as a blacksmith for many years. Esther was a sister to Corda Nelson, whose daughter, Eva, married John Baird in 1935. (Courtesy of KSH.)

Martha Ann Warne sits in the yard with her husband, Thomas Thurman Bennett, at the family farm in Warnetown, located along the boundary of Jefferson and Center Townships. Martha was the eldest of nine Warne children who lived in the area with their families. Her great-grandparents Thomas and Ann Purcell Warne were the first Warnes in Guernsey County, arriving from New Jersey around 1802. (Courtesy of Marilyn Lundquist.)

Thomas Thurman Bennett and Martha Ann Warne married May 11, 1876. They had nine children, however only their six boys survived to adulthood. The entire Bennett family poses for a picture in the early summer of 1914. Shown from left to right are (first row) Robert (Charles's son), Leona (Jim's daughter), Marjory (Otto's daughter), Ruth (Frank's daughter), Katherine (Frank's daughter), Charles (Frank's son), and Harry (Jim's son); (second row) Laura with Martha on her lap, Laura, Ethel, Martha, Doris, Lena, and Cora; (third row) Charles, Irl, Robert, Thomas, Otto, Frank, and Jim. (Courtesy of Barbara Allen.)

The Bennetts lived on a farm at Clio for many years, until they were bought out by the state in the 1950s. This picture of the farm of Emmett Stewart Bennett was taken several years after it was vacated. (Courtesy of Barbara Allen.)

James Orlando Bennett stands to the right of his brother Otto and an unnamed friend out in the woods near Salt Fork Creek. Family members often joked that James thought that he was a real cowboy. (Courtesy of Barbara Allen.)

Mary Elizabeth Warne was the younger sister of Martha Ann Warne, and she married Robert Willis. Their son, Charles Willis (born 1884), utilizes the family buggy in the early 1900s to take himself and his daughter to church. (Courtesy of Marilyn Lundquist.)

Nancy Warne, a sister to Mary Elizabeth and Martha Ann Warne, married Henry Mathers September 29, 1897, and they lived in Center Township for most of their lives. They stand here in front of their house with their two children, Dewey W. and Mary B. (Courtesy of Barbara Allen.)

Mary (born 1900) and Dewey (born 1898) Mathers pose for a portrait in a Cambridge studio in 1902. They were the children of Henry and Nancy Warne Mathers, and they lived their childhoods in the Warnetown portion of Center Township. (Courtesy of Marilyn Lundquist.)

Mildred Lucille Bichard Reed, her infant brother, Don Carlos Bichard, and their great aunt are standing in front of the spring house on the family farm in the early 1930s. The family lived on the farm through the initial years of the Great Depression, from 1929 to 1933. (Courtesy of KSH.)

The Jacob Brower farm was located in the center of Jefferson Township. The property is pictured here from the ridge that overlooked the farm. (Courtesy of Martha Martin.)

Pictured is the James and Grace Cooper farm in the winter of 1930. Grace was the daughter of Mr. Hollingsworth, whose land was sold to the state. The house remained and was later converted to the Sugar Tree Farms Bed and Breakfast. (Courtesy of KSH.)

John Hall holds the hand of his mother, Bessie Hall. Bessie Hall and her husband, John Donald Hall, purchased an 82-acre farm from George Clark in 1930. The Halls could see both the McCleary school and cemetery from their farm house. They could afford one horse and a plow. Later they purchased an old Ford Model T. The state bought the Hall's land in 1966 for the creation of the park. (Courtesy of KSH.)

Floyd and Irene Milligan lived within the Park's boundaries until 1928. They raised corn, hay, and pumpkins, tended sheep and cattle, and kept bees for honey. When they ran low on feed, livestock could subsist on surplus pumpkin. (Courtesy of KSH.)

The Charles "Don" and Merian McWilliams home was built in 1839. They purchased the home from John McKahan in 1955. Prior to the purchase, the McWilliams had lived on the farm of Mr. McWilliams senior. (Courtesy of KSH.)

Three

THE KENNEDY STONE HOUSE

Solomon Sturges received a picturesque tract of land along where the Rocky and Sugar Tree Forks met through a military land grant after the government opened the area to settlers in the early 19th century. He remained on the land until 1837, then sold 80 acres for $100 to Benjamin Kennedy, son of Moses Kennedy, a sheep farmer of Scottish ancestry who had settled near Cadiz. In 1840, Benjamin Kennedy commissioned a local stonemason to build a two-story stone house on the property for him and his wife, Margaret. The Kennedy Stone House would pass through three generations of Kennedy ownership, always to the second child in each generation. The final owner was Don Kennedy, the grandson of Benjamin. Don and his family only lived full time in the house for a limited number of years before moving into Cambridge. They then rented out the house and farm to various tenant farmers until 1966. That year the State of Ohio exercised the right of eminent domain to purchase the 203-acre farm and Stone House from Don Kennedy for the creation of Salt Fork State Park.

The Kennedy Stone House was the only residential structure permitted to remain standing in the course of the construction of the park, though once full-time residents had vacated, the building became only a shell of its former glory. Continuously battered by the elements and subject to vandals, the Kennedy Stone House fell into a sad state of disrepair for many years, as nature fought to reclaim the land. It remained in this condition until March 1999, when Pauline Cornish organized the 10-member Friends of the Kennedy Stone House to restore the magnificent structure and reopen it as a living history museum. With a veteran's memorial courtyard behind the house and a docents' cabin added in 2006, the organization's commitment to protect and preserve the history of the Kennedy Stone House and the families of Jefferson Township has ensured that at least one breathtaking artifact remains to commemorate those who once lived on the lands now known as Salt Fork State Park.

In 1837, Benjamin Franklin Kennedy (1814–1882) and his wife, Margaret Orr Kennedy (1817–1875), purchased an 80-acre tract of land from Solomon Sturges on the Sugar Tree for $100. Benjamin, who was a farmer and later fought for the Union in the Civil War, and Margaret, who was a schoolteacher, had five children together, who were all born on the property. At the time of this image, taken in the summer of 1909, the Kennedy farm consisted of 203 acres. The Sugar Tree Creek flowed benignly through the Kennedy property, where multiple generations of Kennedy children found amusement in its waters. (Courtesy of KSH.)

Three years after purchasing the land, Benjamin commissioned John Little to build a large, two-story stone house on the property for he and his wife for a sum of $500. Little's stonemasons, who where said to have worked barefoot at the site, cut fieldstone into 9 foot by 18 inch blocks for the house. The Kennedy Stone House never had any electricity in it during the time of Kennedy ownership, though Don Kennedy, Benjamin's grandson, did later add a telephone. The house is pictured here in 1940, a century after it was built. (Courtesy of FLHR.)

When Little finished building the Kennedy Stone House, he felt that he had underestimated the project. He offered to build the Kennedys a fruit cellar for an additional $60–$100. Benjamin accepted his offer, and the cellar was built next to the house. (Courtesy of KSH.)

Stone houses were a family tradition for both Benjamin and Margaret Kennedy. Benjamin's grandfather Dr. Samuel Kennedy had a stone house in Tranquility, New Jersey. The house is pictured here in 1935. Margaret's father, Matthew Orr, also had a stone house in Ireland. (Courtesy of KSH.)

Merino sheep, originally from Spain, made the Spanish Empire famous during the 17th and 18th centuries for their sheep and wool production. The Spanish crown tried to restrict their export, but in the 19th century, Napoleon invaded Spain and shared Spain's national treasure with the world. No other wool can compare with the wool of the merino in its color, uniformity, strength, density, and fineness. The sheep have a coating of grease, called lanolin, on its fleece to keep it waterproof. The Kennedy's used to breed and graze these merino sheep on the hill behind their home. (Courtesy of KSH.)

Matthew Tierney Kennedy (1845–1914) was the second oldest son of Benjamin and Margaret Kennedy. He received his common school education at McCleary's Schoolhouse. Matthew was a probationer, rancher, farmer, and mill owner. He spent 18 years traveling and working in California and Montana, where he met Vietta Powers (1854–1938), a schoolteacher in Montana, and he later married her in 1886. The couple had four children: Anna M., Don Philip, Clayton Turney, and Samuel Leland. In October 1877, Matthew purchased the 203-acre Kennedy farm and stone house for $5,000, making him the second generation of Kennedys to own and live in the stone house. (Courtesy of KSH.)

The two eldest children of Matthew and Vietta Kennedy, Don Philip (1888–1970) and Anna M. (1887–1938), pose for a portrait around 1890. Don and Anna, along with their younger brothers, became the second generation of Kennedy children to be born and raised in the stone house. (Courtesy of KSH.)

Seen here, from left to right, Don, Leland, and Clayton Kennedy, the three sons of Matthew and Vietta Kennedy, pose for a picture in the 1920s with the family dog. (Courtesy of KSH.)

Matthew Kennedy's family sits for a portrait in the 1920s. Pictured here left to right are, (first row) Phillip (son of Don), Ethel (daughter of Clayton), Geraldine (daughter of Don), Genevieve (daughter of Anna), Helen (daughter of Clayton), and George (son of Clayton); (second row) Bob (on lap), Florence (wife of Leland), Maud (wife of Clayton), Vietta Kennedy, Anna Kennedy Gaard, and Laura (wife of Don); (third row) Clayton, Leland, and Don. (Courtesy of KSH.)

Anna Kennedy (1887–1938), the only daughter of Matthew and Vietta, married Dr. Christopher Gaard in 1915. Anna gave birth to their daughter, Genevieve Gaard, in 1916. The family stands here with Nick Manner, an air pilot who took them for a ride in his plane in the mid- to late 1920s. (Courtesy of KSH.)

Genevieve Gaard, daughter of Anna Kennedy Gaard, demonstrates her musical talent on the guitar in the family's yard in Jefferson Township around 1930. (Courtesy of KSH.)

Don Phillip Kennedy (1888–1970) was the second child of Matthew Kennedy, and the third and last generation of Kennedys to own the stone house. He was a farmer, a mechanic, and, later, the county commissioner. In 1966, the state purchased the 203-acre Kennedy farm from Don, including the stone house, for $14,000 for the creation of Salt Fork Lake and the park. (Courtesy of FLHR.)

Don Kennedy married Laura Irene McNeel (1894–1961) in the summer 1916. She lived with him at the stone house, where she gave birth to their two children, Geraldine (1917–) and Philip Ralph (1919–1978). Laura was active in the Guernsey County chapter of the Women's Christian Temperance Union, and helped with her husband's campaign to win the county commissioner's seat. Laura succumbed to her battle with breast cancer in 1961, after the family had moved to Cambridge. (Courtesy of KSH.)

Laura Kennedy, like the prior Mrs. Kennedys to live in the stone house, was a schoolteacher in a local school. She stands on the porch of the schoolhouse (back left) with a group of her students. (Courtesy of KSH.)

Geraldine Kennedy (1917–) and Genevieve Gaard (1916–) play in the yard at the Kennedy Stone House with Geraldine's dog, Shep, in 1918–1919. The family's dog was a regular source of summertime entertainment for the two cousins. (Courtesy of KSH.)

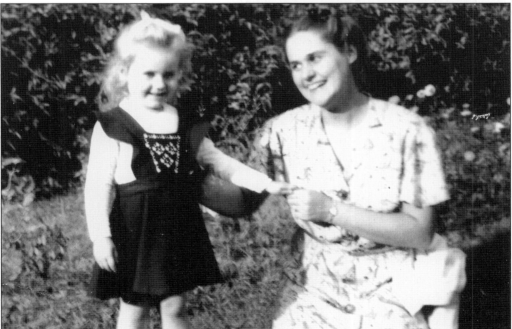

Geraldine Kennedy Keeler kneels in the grass with her daughter, Nancy Keeler, in 1948. Though Geraldine no longer lived at the stone house, she and her family regularly returned to her birthplace for vacations in the summer. (Courtesy of KSH.)

Clayton Turney Kennedy (1891–1971) was the third child of Matthew and Vietta Kennedy. He was a rancher by trade, and in 1917, he married Maud Coley, a schoolteacher. They had three children together, Ethel, George, and Helen. (Courtesy of KSH.)

Ethel Kennedy was the eldest child of Clayton and Maud Kennedy. She is pictured here in July 1935 at the Rackhaaen Camp. (Courtesy of KSH.)

Helen Kennedy Crow, the third child of Clayton and Maud Kennedy, poses for a picture with her infant daughter, Victoria Susan. (Courtesy of KSH.)

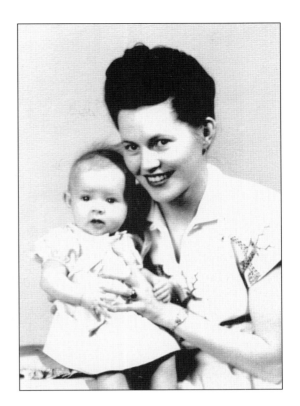

Samuel Leland Kennedy (1894–1942), known simply as Leland, was the fourth child of Matthew and Vietta Kennedy. He married Florence Esther in 1921, and they had two sons, Robert Leland and Joseph Owen. Leland worked as a lawyer, and his father left him an extra $500 in his will due to a physical infirmity. Though Leland was the youngest child, a stroke claimed his life at the age of 47, much before his two older brothers. (Courtesy of KSH.)

Maud Delenia Rachel Kennedy-Clark was the youngest child of Benjamin and Margaret Kennedy, the original owners of the Kennedy Stone House. She married John Barton Clark in 1882, and the couple had four children together. This portrait of her was taken around 1900. (Courtesy of KSH.)

John and Maud Clark's four children pose for a portrait in the 1890s. Seated in front, from left to right, are Etta Frances "Fanny" (1889–1968) and Clarence Leroy "Roy" (1885–1944); standing in the back are Albert Roland "Roll" (1887–1965) and Charles Craig (1884–?). (Courtesy of KSH.)

Charles Craig Clark (1884–?) was the eldest child of John and Maud Clark. In 1912, he married Bessie Jane Zettel, and the couple had no children. He served as a postal worker in Kimbolton in the 1920s. This portrait of Craig was taken in the second decade of the 20th century. (Courtesy of KSH.)

Clarence Leroy "Roy" Clark (1885–1944), the second child of John and Maud Clark, worked as a farmer and a mail carrier. He married Mary Grace Umstott (1887–1950) in 1908. The couple had six children together. Roy and Mary are both buried in Kimbolton. (Courtesy of KSH.)

After the state took possession of the Kennedy Stone House and farm, the buildings fell into disrepair. The many barns on the property were torn down, though a few remaining stones from their foundations still mark their location a short distance from the house. The stone house itself suffered the abuse of the elements and vandals over the years, leaving it in the pictured condition by 1991. (Courtesy of KSH.)

In 1975, the State of Ohio placed the Kennedy Stone House on the National Register of Historic Places. The house's status was indicated by the plaque placed on the boarded up front door, though little attempt was made to protect the house from vandals and the elements. (Courtesy of KSH.)

After the state created the lake, much of the Kennedy property was flooded, though the stone house was saved. The tall pine trees in front of the house were planted around 1900 by Vietta Kennedy, taken as seedlings from her mother's home in Maine. A dock was built in front of the house so that boaters could stop to explore the area. (Courtesy of KSH.)

In March 1999, Pauline Cornish officially organized the Friends of the Kennedy Stone House, whose 10 members sought to repair and preserve the stone house. The house and its interior rooms were restored to the state they had been in during the time it was inhabited by the Kennedys. The lower level contained a dining room and a parlor, and the upstairs housed two bedrooms. The organization also added a kitchen to the back of the house, a replica of the kitchen that Matthew had built for Vietta shortly after the couple moved into the house. (Courtesy of KSH.)

The Kennedy Stone House currently serves as a window to the past, with artifacts and tools that earlier residents of the region would have used in the course of their lives. (Courtesy of KSH.)

The Kennedy Stone House hosts living history days, where people dress in the clothing from a specified time period and perform the activities that would have been typical for their gender from the particular era. (Courtesy of KSH.)

Four

SCHOOLS, CHURCHES, AND BRIDGES

The stories of the past remain stored in the structures that attended them. The sturdy structures that adorn the human landscape preserve them as nobly as old books. Perhaps the greatest loss suffered with the creation of the park was the disappearance of these vessels of memory. These images, preserved by the people who once lived here, can help preserve those stories of a lost community, by serving as visual prompts for personal, family, and neighborhood memories. A covered bridge recalls a late spring day spent fishing while bare feet dangle off its edge; an old church evokes the sounds of "Amazing Grace" or "Bless Be the Tie that Binds" carried through the window on a warm summer Sunday; the schoolhouse bell tower brings out a memory of old classmates and beloved teachers. Most of the structures pictured in this chapter have vanished from the landscape. The authors hope that their reproduction here will prompt a thousand stories from the tongues of past residents, stories that might be passed down the generations.

The Armstrong School House was named after the nearby family, the Armstrongs. This Jefferson Township schoolhouse was located near Clio, where Armstrong's Mill operated at one time. Some of the teachers included Campsa Robe, Lenna McGrew, W. G. Ingram, Harry Bishard, Ray McCracken, Guy Harding, Glenn Peoples, Gail Addy, Laura McNeel, Olive Bell, Margaret Kirkwood, Lucille Jenkins, and Bernadine Jenkins. (Courtesy of GCHS.)

The Grandridge School, located in Madison Township, takes a class picture in the early 1930s. Pictured left to right are (first row) Hervey Eagleson, Edmond Eagleson, Charles A., Adell Garet, unidentified, John Eagleson, and Walter Eagleson; (second row) Georgia Nicholas, Jerome Adkins, Willard Paden, Paul Paden, Raymond Paden, Stewart Nicholas, and Frances Nicholas. (Courtesy of Clifford Eagelson.)

The school at Cross Roads was located in Jefferson Township, half-way between Center and Winterset. This building was used as a schoolhouse from 1853 to 1949, until it changed school districts into Madison Township. At one time the school bus was driven by Ray Gibson. (Courtesy of GCHS.)

School picnics were a great way to end the school year for the pupils. This picnic was the spring picnic for the Cross Roads School, which was located at what is now the main entrance to the park along Route 22. The children pictured here, from left to right, are Homer Bichard, Jerry Cowgill, Brownie Hill, Larry Bell, Marlene Bell, and Janice Allen. Identified behind them are Jossie Chome, Roy Allen, Gus Fedrick, Duris Allen, and Alice Cowgill. (Courtesy of KSH.)

Pictured here are the students of Cross Roads School in 1948–1949. Identified here are Connie Jenkins, Phyllis Miller, Barbara Watkins, Lois Carter, Mr. Johnson, Dallas Gregory, Sue Triplett, Barbara Johns, Carol Gunn, Bonnie Powell, Shirley Warne Beverly Watkins, Glada Johnson, Mary Martin, Glena Triplett, Mary Carter, teacher Blanch Tedrick, and Richard Jenkins. (Courtesy of Roy and Garnett Carter family.)

The Birmingham High School class of 1928–1929 stands on the steps of the schoolhouse. Identified here are Virginia Foster, Dorothy Beale, Grace McCleary, Eva Hollingsworth Parker, Don Braniger, Grace Jones, Mary Smith, Nedra Pickering, Emitt Waryck (the principal), Kenneth Akins, Raymond Willis, Margaret Jones, John Foster, John Willis Parker and Carl Combs. (Courtesy of FLHM.)

John Willis Parker and Eva Hollingsworth Parker returned to Birmingham High School in 1982, the place where their romance first started. The couple was married in 1933, and they celebrated their 70th wedding anniversary in 2003. Their son, Charlie Parker, penned the poem *It all Began in Birmingham* in honor of the occasion. (Courtesy of Charlie Parker.)

Kimbolton School was a two-room building located in Kimbolton, Liberty Township. Kimbolton was a typical schoolhouse with typical expectations for teachers. Some duties that teachers were required to perform were "to follow the Course of Study, making careful preparation for each day's work, to have immediate care of the school. Teachers must be in their respective school rooms for the ringing of the first bell. They must devote their entire time to the schools and not dismiss until the final closing hour." (Courtesy of Barbara Allen.)

Knob School was named after the fact that it stood near the top of a hill. It was also nicknamed Devils-Knob because of the controversy about where to place the new school. The students would take hikes to celebrate Arbor Day. They would swing on grapevines, pick wild flowers, and then return to school. There was no water available at the school, so it had to be carried in from a nearby homestead. Regardless of the weather, all students were expected to attend. At recess, students played games such as prisoner's base, tag, anteover, and ball. Some teachers included Anna McKahan, Glenn Peoples, Watt Banker, Pearl Yarnell, Laura McNeel, Audrey Allender, and Alma Ford McCance. (Courtesy of GCHS.)

A selection of the Knob School students in Jefferson Township in 1926 is shown here. Pictured from left to right are (first row) Mansel Gibson, unidentified, Freda Gibson, and Ward Bishard; (second row) Nilva Gibson, Evalyn Stricklin, Mildred Bishard, and Ralph Bishard. (Courtesy of Martha Martin.)

One year later in 1927, the Knob student body included, from left to right, (first row) Ward Bishard and Eileen Wayt; (second row) Mildred Bishard, Ralph Bishard, Kathleen Wayt, Evelyn Stricklin. (Courtesy of Martha Martin.)

North Salem School house stood in Liberty Township. Some of its teachers included Corda Nelson, Craig Thompson, George Bell, Walter Bell, George Berry, and Edward Bell. (Courtesy of GCHS.)

Corda Nelson was a schoolteacher at several one-room schoolhouses located in and around Jefferson Township, including the schools at North Salem, Bird's Run, Kimbolton, Rock Town Hill, and Paterys Trap. (Courtesy of KSH.)

Ernest Earl Duhamell is pictured here at 10 years old and in the fourth grade. He was a pupil of Nelson's while she taught at North Salem. Written on the back of his school picture was "October 1924. To my teacher Corda Nelson. Remember me when this you see, I will remember you." (Courtesy of John Baird.)

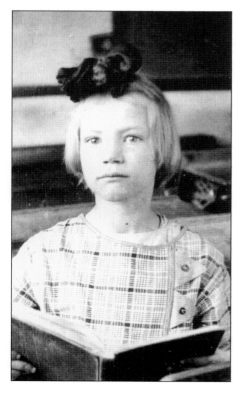

Ernest's sister, Lillian Ruth Duhamell, also attended North Salem schoolhouse. This picture was also taken in October 1924, while she was in the second grade and was eight years old. She writes, "To my teacher Corda Nelson. I will remember you Teacher, think of me in after years." (Courtesy of John Baird.)

Independence, or Possum Glory, schoolhouse sat on Larrick Ridge, which is north of Route 40. The building was then owned by Ira Nelson. The road in front of the school led to Wolf's Den. Teachers included Mayme Hunt. It was later closed when Knob school opened because it was more central for area families. (Courtesy of GCHS.)

Pictured here are the students of Independence School during the 1910–1911 school year. It was taken on November 22, 1910. (Courtesy of GCHS.)

Odell, otherwise known as Berwick, was a one-room schoolhouse located close to Hosak's Cave in Monroe Township. One year, the enrollment included 10 students, 6 of whom were from one family. Some of its teachers included Mrs. Ora Miller and Lida McCullough. (Courtesy of GCHS.)

Wilmer Taylor taught at Odell for many years. He is pictured here with his students. (Courtesy of Lori Taylor.)

McCleary schoolhouse was named after the family that donated the land for the school. They also owned a mill that sat near the Sugar Tree Fork. Forrest Combs recalled that in addition to his teacher duties, he did his own janitorial work. He taught all eight grades at the school. Other teachers included Lucille Anderson, Pearl Gibson, Gladys Ford, Leon Mallet, and Dana Lawrence. (Courtesy of GCHS.)

Salt Fork schoolhouse was located on former County Road 45. The property was bought in 1878 by the Liberty Township Board of Education and was closed in 1940. Some of the duties that students were expected to perform were "To have a particular desk assigned by the teacher and keep it, as well as the floor beneath it, in a neat and orderly condition." (Courtesy of GCHS.)

Seminary School was located in Monroe Township. One of its teachers was Annie Warden. (Courtesy of GCHS.)

Sugar Tree School convened very near Sugar Tree Fork. Forrest Dryden-Combs retells a story about how his mother, Cloma Beal, met his father, Raleigh Dryden. She was a young student at the school, when a romance developed between her and her teacher. They would pass notes to each other by using her books that he would borrow and then read from. Other students never noticed the romance. They were married on November 28, 1906, and then Raleigh died less than a year later in June 1907. Cloma recalls that she was married, widowed and became mother all in her 17th year. Teachers included Raleigh Dryden, Gladys Ford, Isaac Ross Jenkins, and Sylvester Patterson. (Courtesy of GCHS.)

The Sugar Tree School class of 1896 poses for a picture. Identified here are John Smith, Eva Kimball, Roy Fordyce, Cloma Beal, Lon Lanning, Maggie Beal, Harry Stiles, Leona Stiles, Otho Stiles, Minnie Stiles, Ethel Laning, Frank Beal, Daisy Parker, Maggie Kimball, John Fordyce, Nettie Parker, Beryl Taylor, Ella Kimball, Frank Bonnell, Charlie Kimball, Lixxie Redd, Frank Stiles, Florence Fordyce, Ed Taylor, Fannie Stiles, John Beal, Cora Fordyce, Ross Willis, John Stiles, Will Willis, Fannie Parker, Mart Combs, Ollie Beal, Will Stiles, Wilbur Beal, Annie Beal, Harry Fordyce, Will Combs, Hayes Taylor, Melvin Fordyce, Austin Bonnell (teacher), George Stiles (former city mail carrier), Charlie Parker, and Milton Stiles (former city auditor). (Courtesy of Charlie Parker.)

Allen's Church, pictured here in 1941, was the first church organized in Jefferson Township in 1824. It was originally held in William Allen's home, who had been the fourth person to settle in the township in 1805. The first meetinghouse was built in 1839, on land that Allen had deeded to the church. (Courtesy of KSH.)

Allen's Church later became the Valley Grange Meeting Hall No. 1586. When Salt Fork Lake was constructed, the state tore down the old church building. Its foundation stones can still be seen on the side of Road 14. (Courtesy of KSH.)

Center Baptist Church was organized in 1832 and built in 1835. In 1966, the property was sold to Valley Grange, and they used it for the Grand Hall. The church changed denominations many times during its lifetime. A rivalry arose between this parish and the Methodist church just a few plots away. Once a choir member got mad and left the Baptist church and became a Methodist. Today the church still stands on Route 22 and has a lively congregation. (Courtesy of GCHS).

Center Methodist Church was built in 1858. In the beginning, the church only met once every week, on a weeknight, because that was the only time that a preacher was available to come. Annual events at the church included Easter Sunrise Service, Cantatas, Mother Daughter Banquets, and Christmas Eve Candlelight Service. Center Methodist is still located in Center Township along Route 22. John Lanning claims that when he was young, he and his friends were playing baseball one spring in the 1950s and knocked all the windows out. The next morning, Easter morning, the windows had to be boarded up with cardboard. (Courtesy of GCHS.)

The Clear Fork United Presbyterian Church in Monroe Township was organized as an associate church in 1835. Pastors for the church included James McGill, J. C. Brownlee, A. C. Reid, David Thompson, Samuel McArthur, J. W. Martin, and J. T. Campbell. After nearly a century in existence, the church was closed in the early 1930s. (Courtesy of GCHS.)

Irish Ridge Methodist was located in Monroe Township. The church is now a United Methodist church and is still standing today. The Kennedy family of the Kennedy Stone House attended Irish Ridge Methodist and many members of the family were buried there. (Courtesy of GCHS.)

This picture of Millers Methodist was taken in October 1949. At the time, the church stood in Wills Township, but has been since torn down. (Courtesy of FLHR.)

Tyner Methodist Church was located a mile from the dam in Liberty Township. In 1936, the church had 25 members, and their pastor was Ivan Bartrug, who also conducted services at the Kimbolton and Birds Run Methodist churches. (Courtesy of GCHS.)

Pleasant Hill United Presbyterian Church was built in 1867. At one time, the church had a very large congregation and held picnics and reunions. It was the last remaining church in Jefferson Township. It was torn down around 1985. The trustees bought the building from the Presbyterian Church for $1 after the church closed in 1976–1977. The building was located at the end of Candy Road, on the outskirts of Salt Fork Park. The church was built next to Pleasant Hill Cemetery, which was established before 1822. This cemetery also has a soldier buried in it from nearly every American War. Some of the soldiers are listed here—War of 1812: John Marling, Richard and John Cornell; the U.S.–Mexican War: David Lytle; the Civil War: David Lytle, James M. Beggs, James M. Nelson, Emmett S. Bennett, James Burnsworth, and Joseph Bower; the Spanish-American War: Raymond F. Weidmer; World War I: Byron K. Gillespie. (Courtesy of GCHS.)

Here is the Pleasant Hill Cemetery as it stands today, without the church. The graves of the Allen Cemetery were relocated here when the park was built. (Courtesy of William Kerrigan.)

In 1881, the Methodists of Winterset built a new church to accommodate their growing population. They bought lot 18 from A. F. Lynn for $75. This site is now along Route 22, or Cadiz Road. The building cost about $2,000 and was built by J. B. Lydick and the Sons of Quaker City. The building only had two stoves, which were the only source of heat for the building. Over the years, many programs have been run, including Bible school, revivals, Bible studies, and fund-raisers. The building even endured a fire on January 26, 1975. (Courtesy of GCHS.)

Current and past members of the Winterset Methodist church gathered in August of 2006 for their annual homecoming celebration. (Courtesy of William Kerrigan.)

The worshippers at North Salem United Presbyterian Church, located in Liberty Township, originally met in a log building built near Miller's Mill in 1836, until the actual church building was constructed in 1850. Early pastors included John Anderson, Alexander Miller, James Duncan, William Johnston, W. C. Sommers, J. W. Martin, J. C. Hammond, and J. S. McMunn. The church is still active today. (Courtesy of GCHS.)

The Allen's Chapel Bridge, located near Allen's Church in Jefferson Township, spanned the Salt Fork Creek until 1936, when the structure was removed. The only thing remaining to mark the area where it once stood is a large pine tree that sat in Old Allen's Cemetery, which can be seen near the water still today. (Courtesy of GCHS.)

The covered bridge on State Highway 285 in Madison Township, also known as the Salt Fork Bridge, is reputed to be the site where Confederate general Morgan and Union general Shackelford met under a flag of truce during the Civil War, after the two forces had engaged in a brief battle in old Washington. The truce was merely a ruse to allow General Morgan's troops time to escape, and General Shackelford was forced to pursue General Morgan through Winterset and Antrim, before finally catching him near the West Virginia border. The bridge collapsed around 1937, under the heavy weight of a tractor, and locals from the area assisted in the clean up. Standing to the left are Harry Johnson, Eddie Eagleson, Cliff Eagleson, Clearance Johnson, and Donald Eagleson, along with two unidentified men in the back. (Courtesy of Clifford Eagleson.)

The Armstrong Bridge crossed Salt Fork Creek approximately five miles northeast of Cambridge in Jefferson Township. It was located near the once busy and thriving crossroads town of Clio. Abraham Armstrong was hired by the county in 1849 to build the covered bridge for the Armstrong gristmill and sawmill at Clio for $510. The date of construction made the bridge one of the oldest in Ohio, and rather than destroying it with the construction of Salt Fork Lake, the structure was moved to the Cambridge City Park in the winter of 1966–1967, where it remains today. (Courtesy of Finley Local History Room.)

Today the Armstrong Bridge has been relocated to the Cambridge City Park, where it spans a small creek along a pedestrian trail. (Photograph by William Kerrigan.)

The McCleary Mill Bridge, named for the family's sawmill and gristmill located nearby, bridged the Sugar Tree Creek two miles southeast of North Salem. It was built sometime in the mid-1800s with the help of David McCullough, and it was said to have been 12 to 14 inches higher on one end than the other. In August 1957, the wooden structure was replaced by a bridge of steel construction. (Courtesy of GCHS.)

The Milligan Bridge spanned Sugar Tree Creek two miles south of North Salem in Liberty Township, and it was the second bridge erected in this site. The first bridge was named McMullen Bridge. The bridge was one of four covered bridges slated to be disassembled or demolished to make way for Salt Fork Lake, but in 1966, the bridge was burned by vandals.

The Tyner "Narrows" Covered Bridge crossed Wills Creek at the junction of the Salt Fork, making the structure a target of flood waters from both streams for the century that it stood. It was built in the 1850s, with a cost exceeding $500 and was originally known as the Miller Bridge, due to the five Miller families living in the area. The main span of the bridge was 85 feet long, making it one of the longer covered bridges in Guernsey County. In later years, it had to be anchored to nearby trees with a cable to keep it from being carried away by flood waters. The bridge was replaced after 100 years of service in 1955 by a steel and concrete structure. (Courtesy of GCHS.)

The Warne Covered Bridge crossed Salt Fork Creek at the very southern portion of Jefferson Township on the Ed Yaus property, near the area known as Warnetown, or Warrentown. Yaus married a Warne girl before moving to the property. Yaus was a fox hunter who owned black and tan dogs, and his dogs walked in front of his horse when he traveled. (Courtesy of FLHR.)

The Gunn Bridge, which was flooded by the waters of the Sugar Tree Creek in 1967, was located three and a half miles east of North Salem in Jefferson Township. Efforts to save the bridge from the construction of Salt Fork Lake failed, and the waters of the reservoir rose up around the structure, though a portion of the trusses can still be seen above the waters today. (Courtesy of FLHR.)

The Gunn Bridge remained standing after the waters of Sugar Tree Fork rose in 1967. The structure eventually collapsed into the water, where it lay unnoticed by most passers-by. When the lake levels were lowered in the summer of 2005 in order to repair the dam, much of the structure of the old Gunn Bridge re-emerged. (Courtesy of The Daily Jeffersonian.)

Five

THE LAKE

In the post–World War II years, life changed quickly for the region's small farmers. External forces were having a profound effect on their way of life. Technological innovations in agriculture and improved transportation networks created economies that favored large, sometimes distant farms over smaller, local ones. In the early 1960s, the construction of two interstates through the area, as well as dramatic improvements in local roadways, brought the country closer to the city and accelerated the demise of the rural general store. As the population declined in the Salt Fork region, the dream of creating a lake and park grew. By the 1960s, the state began acquiring land for the creation of what would become Ohio's largest state park. Families left tidy farmsteads, lovingly cultivated for generations, with heavy hearts as the state began constructing a dam and dismantling old homes and barns. In 1969, the dam was completed and the water rose quickly, as contractors and construction crews raced to complete the magnificent lodge and other park facilities. Crews worked year round in rugged conditions to get the work done. In 1972, Salt Fork Lodge was opened to the public.

Over the last 35 years, millions have come to the park annually to enjoy its natural beauty. The signs of the land's past quickly faded as the forests grew. But in 2005, the past made a brief reappearance, when the state dropped water levels five feet in order to repair the dam. Old roadbeds and other artifacts of the past returned to view. In parts of the park, the serpentine paths of the original creeks reappeared. By 2006, rains had refilled the lake, but tell-tale clues of the past are still visible if one knows where to look.

PARKER FARM AUCTION
WINTERSET, OHIO
SATURDAY, SEPT. 10, 1966
10:00 A. M. E. S. T.
LOCATED 2½ MI. N.W. OF WINTERSET, O. OFF U.S. ROUTE 22
ON GUERNSEY CO. RD. 47

218 SHEEP
Selling an old established flock of purebred black-top Delaine sheep. They have been highly selected for lamb production and pounds of quality wool and include: 11 Targhee ewes, 8 Dorset Delaine ewe lambs, 20 Delaine ewe lambs, 15 Delaine yearling ewes, 38 Delaine 2 and 3 yr. olds, 54 Delaine 4 and 5 yr. old ewes, 68 aged ewes, 2 Delaine rams, 2 Suffolk rams.

FARM EQUIPMENT
Farmall C tractor, cultivators, and double 14 inch mounted plows; Bennett loader for Ford or Ferguson tractor; N.I. 95 bu. tractor spreader; N.H. No. 66 baler with motor; N.I. ground driven hay rake; N.H. 7 ft. 3-point mower (like new); 6 ft. double disc; J.D. 3-point p.t.o. corn sheller; two farm wagons with grain box; Mayrath 30 ft. hay and grain conveyer; Co-op 13 disc grain drill; 8 ft. double cultipacker; Co-op single row corn picker; ele. corn sheller; Chatam seed cleaner; 3-point field sprayer; hand fodder chopper; tractor buzz saw; hog feeders and waterers; extension ladders; chicken equipment; egg washer; platform scales; log chains; wagon tongues; hand tools; scrap pile; misc. items.

COLLECTORS ITEMS
Sleigh; picture frames; glassware and dishes; stone jugs and jars; rockers; iron kettles; fireplace kettles; grain cradle; block planes; large farm wagon wheels; saddles, western and side; two horse spring wagon; curved glass china closet; sleigh bells. (First auction on the premises for 5 generations.)

HOUSEHOLD GOODS
Seigler 75,000 b.t.u. gas space heater, fully automatic and like new; Tappan gas range; Manitowoc deep freeze; kneehold desk; dropleaf mahogany dining table and 4 chairs; lounge chair; Philco radio; platform rocker; floor and table lamps; two piece dining room suite; wall couch; matching coffee and end tables; stands; upright piano; magazine racks; 2 beds with springs; 2 dressers; chairs; mirrors; drapes; rugs (room size and scatter); two chrome dinette sets; fruit jars; porch swing; other items.

1000 Bale Mixed Hay
100 Bale Straw

Lunch Stand

HERBERT A. BAMBECK
Complete Auction Service
R. 1, DOVER, OHIO 44622

MR. AND MRS. J. WILLIS PARKER, Owners
R. 1, Lore City, Ohio

By the mid-1960s, Salt Fork families were packing their belongings and preparing to move. Flyers like this one told a common story, as families, some who had resided on the same land for five generations, sold off what they could not take with them. Some purchased new land nearby and continued to farm; others moved into towns like Cambridge or moved farther away. This handbill from the Parker family auction offers a small glimpse into the ordeal of Salt Fork's displaced families. (Courtesy of Charlie Parker.)

A view of Sugar Tree Fork, just before the creation of the lake, is seen here. Old Rocky Fork Road extends from the left side of the photograph into the background. Looking at this view today, one would see the North Salem Boat launch in the background. (Courtesy of Salt Fork State Park.)

Parker Road still crosses Brushy Creek in the eastern part of the park. The road was named for the Parker family, the first white settlers on this piece of land. The Parkers also built a tidy farm north of here, where Parker Road crosses the eastern reaches of Sugar Tree Fork. This part of the park's land remains above water, and the now paved Parker Road leads to some of the park's best birding and hunting areas. (Courtesy of Salt Fork State Park.)

In order prepare the bottom lands for the lake, work crews cleared and burned some trees. Notice the pile of burned logs just behind the diesel tank. This view is probably from the lake bottom, near the dam, looking toward what is now Morning Glory boat launch. Contractors working on all parts of park construction worked in difficult conditions. This red gas drum was used to fill up equipment when the lake was being made. (Courtesy of Salt Fork State Park.)

Several small temporary dams like this one were created to hold back the flow of water from feeder streams during the construction of Salt Fork Dam. (Courtesy of Salt Fork State Park.)

Contractors raced to finish building construction as the water quickly rose. Here is a view of the lodge from the rising water as it was being completed. Today, new forest covers all of the cleared area. (Courtesy of Salt Fork State Park.)

Luburgh Construction received the contract to build the magnificent $5.5 million lodge, described as the finest park lodge in the nation at that time. With 148 guest rooms and 74,237 square feet of space, it was built to accommodate the large numbers of visitors the park would receive. The lodge was opened in May 1972. (Courtesy of Salt Fork State Park.)

Cal and Harold Davis owned Davis Construction Company, Inc., during the construction of Salt Fork State Park, and their company was contracted by Luburgh Excavating to build various structures throughout the park, including the bathing complex, all the restrooms, the water treatment plant, and the campground entry office. They had anywhere from 20 to 24 local men working on their construction crew during their three years there, and since there were no established power lines in the park, they had to run all of their equipment off of generators. In addition to buildings, the company did all the concrete work for Luburgh Excavating, including the pouring of beach walls that extended four feet down into the ground. The crew working on this, pictured here in 1969, included, from left to right, Fred "Slim" Tedrick, Wilbur "Squib" Hess, Jim Potts, Andy Zahela, and Bob Yearian. (Courtesy of Harold Davis.)

Longtime Salt Fork resident Carl Allen stands on the beams of the new park bridge, which crosses the lake just north of the park office. The Allens were among the first families to settle in Jefferson Township, and farmed the adjoining lands for generations. (Courtesy of Carl Allen.)

Governor Rhodes delivers the keynote address at the dedication ceremony for Salt Fork State Park. (Courtesy of Carl Allen.)

The ground breaking ceremony for the lodge in 1969 was an exciting event for Guernsey County's leaders. Pictured here, from left to right, are Dave Brooks, President of Bank One; Bob Amos; James Scott, Guernsey County prosecutor; John Tingler, mayor of Cambridge; Ellis McCracken; Fred E. Morr, head of Ohio Department of Natural Resources; Tom Bowlin; Everett Reese; and Evelyn Bruney. (Courtesy of Carl Allen.)

Rangers Don Vincent (left) and Willard McCauley pose by the entrance to the new park. Note the land on the hill behind them is all cleared, as was about 70 percent of the parkland at the time of construction. Today this hillside is covered in new forest. Old U.S. Route 22 traversed the top of this ridge before this cut was made for the new road. The location is also near the site of the old Crossroads School, but earth moving and road construction at the park entrance have removed all evidence of its presence. (Courtesy of Salt Fork State Park.)

Today the once fertile bottom lands of Salt Fork yield more muskies rather than maize, and walleyes rather than wool. The lake buzzes with activity on weekends, but it is still not difficult to find silence and serenity in the middle of the week. (Courtesy of Salt Fork State Park.)

In 2005, state engineers discovered a small boil at the base of the dam. The Ohio Department of Natural Resources assessed the situation quickly, and ordered repairs. Although the engineers concluded there was no eminent danger to communities below the dam, the water level was lowered five feet during the repair process. Director of the Ohio Department of Natural Resources Sam Speck (center) and assistant director Glen Alexander look on, as two unidentified engineers use a piezometer to measure seepage in the dam. (Courtesy of The Daily Jeffersonian.)

The lowering of the lake level by five feet in the summer of 2005 revealed a world that had not been seen for 35 years. This basin behind the park headquarters is broad and shallow when the water is up, and a perfect place to fish for catfish. Here the original meandering streambed of Salt Fork Lake is exposed temporarily. Fishermen take note. (Courtesy of Salt Fork State Park.)

The lowering of the lake level also exposed many roadbeds partially or completely hidden from view. This is the roadbed of old U.S. Route 22, just east of the park entrance, looking east. (Courtesy of David Thompson.)

Ben Baker (left) and David Thompson take a stroll on old road to Linn's Mill, hidden from view today, but dry as a bone in the summer of 2005. The road leads up to the site of the old Linn's Mill. An old millstone is still visible along the shoreline in the background. (Photograph by Tara Thompson.)

Six

Exploring Salt Fork State Park

The past is still present at Salt Fork State Park. Not just in the living history programs at the restored Kennedy Stone House, but atop every hill and down every hollow, evidence of those who made a life here in the past can still be found. All that is required to discover it is a keen eye, a little physical exertion, and a sense of adventure. This last chapter will provide you with a few tips for setting out on your own historical detective trip. While some of these markers of the past can be reached by car or motorboat, the quieter, slower pace of walking, biking, paddling, or horseback riding are more suited for discovery. Knowing where to look and what to look for will also help. Pick up some maps of the park at the headquarters and compare them to the map provided in this book. Then choose a trail or waterway and set out.

1870 Plat Map of the Salt Fork Region, with a map of the lake superimposed on top.

114

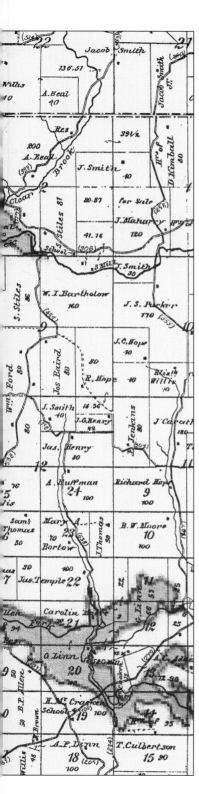

This map provides a rough overlay of Salt Fork Lake on an 1870 plat map of Jefferson Township, and parts of Liberty, Center, and Madison Townships. Comparing it to a modern map, you will see that some, but not all, of the park's roads follow roads cuts by the early settlers. Also note the small squares indicating structures. At many of these locations, one will still find sandstone foundations today. If one is interested in tracking down an old family homestead from a different time period, one can find many historic plat maps of the county at the Guernsey County map room and the Finley Local History room at the main library in Cambridge. (Map constructed by William Kerrigan.)

Note how the Allen house is framed by two large Norway Spruce trees in this old photograph of the Allen home. The Norway Spruce is not a native tree, but it has been an immensely popular front yard tree since the late 19th century. As one explores the park, keep an eye out for especially large specimens. They are the best first clues to finding the locations of old homesteads. (Courtesy of Carl Allen.)

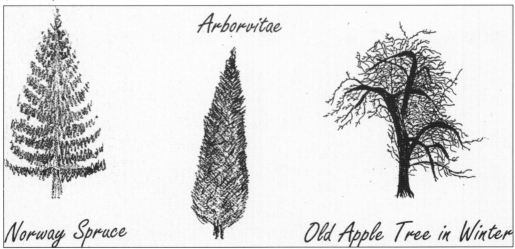

Arborvitae

Norway Spruce

Old Apple Tree in Winter

While the towering Norway Spruce is the easiest to spot, there are other trees to look for that will help direct one to old foundations. Extraordinarily large oaks, maples, and willows predate the park and were often found in front yards; the southern Catalpa tree was also popular. Arborvitae is not as long lived, but many yard-planted specimens are still in the park. Finally, gnarly old apple trees, and some peach trees (most no longer bearing) were planted not too far from old farmhouses. (Drawing by William Kerrigan.)

Once an old foundation or graveyard has been found, a closer view also reveals other lingering signs of the human past. The popular shade-loving ground cover vinca spreads like a carpet around many old foundations and cemeteries; naturalized daylilies and daffodils are also common, as is trumpet vine. Lilac bushes often survive the growth of the forest, but stop flowering. They can be identified by their leaves. An unwelcome guest is also found nearby—poison ivy. One must be sure to wear protective clothing when venturing into the woods. (Courtesy of William Kerrigan.)

Vinca and daylilies surround this old house foundation, on the site of the 1870 Henry farm. An old wrought-iron bed remains within the sandstone walls. These places should be treated with the respect they deserve. Leave only footprints, take only pictures. (Courtesy of William Kerrigan.)

117

An old outhouse remains, barely standing, on the site of the Dave Scott farm. New Concord pharmacist Kent Pattison recalls visiting the farm when he was a boy. The Scotts never had indoor plumbing, electricity, a car, or a tractor, and relied primarily on human and horse power to earn a living from the land. (Courtesy of William Kerrigan.)

The Scotts did, however, have a crank phone, and used a small windmill to charge the battery that ran it. They called the neighbor by turning the crank a few times, and arranged for a ride into town when they needed one. This unusually straight "tree," now sits deep in the woods, and is easy to miss if one is not looking for it. It was the one modern amenity on the Scott's rural farm. (Courtesy of William Kerrigan.)

Kent Pattison recalls refusing to enter the Scott's home during his visit, as an extremely large hornet's nest hung from an apple tree just near this door. Besides the outhouse and main house foundation, remnants of the well, the smokehouse, the pigpen, and the barn are still visible. The GPS coordinates for locating this site are at the end of this book. (Courtesy of William Kerrigan.)

The ruins of another homestead are not far from the Buckeye Trail in the eastern part of the park. Remants of several structures, and other rusted relics from the early 20th century, are still present. (Courtesy of William Kerrigan.)

In late summer and fall, Salt Fork's apple trees show off their fruit. Some are old orchard trees, made unruly by neglect; others are their wilder offspring, sprung from seeds. Both point toward the agrarian past. Pluck an apple from an old tree and take a bite if you have the courage. As Henry David Thoreau wrote in his essay *Wild Apples*, "They belong to children as wild as themselves, —to certain active boys I know, —to the wild-eyed woman of the fields, to whom nothing comes amiss, who gleans after all to the world, and, moreover, to us walkers." (Courtesy of William Kerrigan.)

Black locust was prized by farmers for making fence posts. Its reputation for longevity is well earned, as lines of locust fence posts still mark the boundaries of old farm fields. (Courtesy of William Kerrigan.)

The crumbling blacktop of this old county road, numbered 96 on the 1870 plat map, is still evident along the peninsula that divides Rocky Fork from Sugar Tree Fork. The road now ends where it meets the mouth of Rocky Fork. Remnants of an old crossroads village and several house foundations can be found along the road. The site is only reachable by boat or horse trail. The trail starts in the parking lot near Hosak's Cave. (Courtesy of William Kerrigan.)

Not far from any house foundation, you'll usually find the place the residents discarded household goods no longer needed. Broken pottery, old soda and medicine bottles, and other items offer the explorer a glimpse into the lives of the residents. (Courtesy of William Kerrigan.)

Some of the best discoveries can be made traveling by canoe or kayak. The slow, deliberate pace of a human-powered vessel reveals things unseen by those motoring by. Here near the site of old Linn's Mill (see image on page 17), an old broken millstone lies partially buried along the shore. (Courtesy of William Kerrigan.)

The shoreline is also the best place to find the remnants of old roads and bridges. Old bricks and sandstone litter the shoreline at the point the road up to the old Scott house meets the lake. From here, one can follow the old roadbed on foot along a steep and scenic gorge to the remains of the old Scott farm. (Courtesy of William Kerrigan.)

A few pieces of wood rising above the water on Sugar Tree Fork appear to be nothing more than tree stumps from a distance. Up close however, one can see that these timbers are squared, and still contain hardware. This is all that remains visible of the old Gunn Bridge when the lake is high (also seen in the top image on page 102). (Courtesy of William Kerrigan.)

Are there hay bales in the park? A few small parcels of parkland are still farmed, under cooperative agreements with local farmers. This practice actually has tremendous benefits for wildlife, creating landscape diversity and edge environments where game can thrive. This land was part of the old Landman farm. (Courtesy of William Kerrigan.)

Several cemeteries remain within the boundaries of the park. The largest of these, McCleary's Cemetery, is accessible by boat along the Sugar Tree Fork, between the Marina and the Kennedy Stone House, or by trail from the Kennedy Stone House. This stone, almost hidden by the vinca, rests in the Warne Cemetery, accessible to only the most intrepid bushwhackers. (Courtesy of William Kerrigan.)

Authors Alicia Seng and Meredith Bowman had great fun searching for the old Ford Cemetery in the middle of the park. The cemetery is accessible by walking along mown paths, but is not easy to find without the aid of a GPS device. (Courtesy of William Kerrigan.)

The gravestones of infants are often marked with a resting lamb, as is this one in the Warne cemetery. (Courtesy of William Kerrigan.)

A young explorer documents his trip to the Warne cemetery. (Courtesy of William Kerrigan.)

This double spring is still visible along the side of Park Road 52 (Courtesy of William Kerrigan.)

An old wrought iron headboard still stands defiantly in the middle of the old Henry house foundation off Park Road 57. This road now ends into a marsh, but once continued south across Brushy Fork to the site of Linn's Mill, before meeting old U.S. Route 22. (Courtesy of William Kerrigan.)

GPS LOCATIONS

Remnants of the human past at Salt Fork—from house, school, and bridge foundations to old cemeteries and hidden roads—can still be found throughout the park. These GPS headings can get you started. More details can be found at www.geocaching.com.

Reachable by car with minimal walking:
Pleasant Hill Cemetery	N40.05.334 W081.31.235
Double Spring	N40.07.030 W081.28.677
Henry Homestead	N40.06.646 W081.27.515

Reachable by water, may also require some walking:
Linn's millstone	N40.05.312 W081.27.467
Adams homestead	N40.08.063 W081.30.444
McCleary homestead	N40.08.119 W081.29.539
Gunn Bridge remnants	N40.07.955 W081.29.097
McCleary Cemetery	N40.07.586 W081.30.614

Requires some hiking:
Scott homestead	N40.06.521 W081.30.967
Ford Cemetery	N40.07.479 W081.28.757
Homestead along the Buckeye Trail	N40.07.037 W081.27.239

Requires some bushwhacking:
Warne Cemetery	N40.04.166 W081.29.574

ACROSS AMERICA, PEOPLE ARE DISCOVERING SOMETHING WONDERFUL. *THEIR HERITAGE.*

Arcadia Publishing is the leading local history publisher in the United States. With more than 3,000 titles in print and hundreds of new titles released every year, Arcadia has extensive specialized experience chronicling the history of communities and celebrating America's hidden stories, bringing to life the people, places, and events from the past. To discover the history of other communities across the nation, please visit:

www.arcadiapublishing.com

Customized search tools allow you to find regional history books about the town where you grew up, the cities where your friends and family live, the town where your parents met, or even that retirement spot you've been dreaming about.